ECHOES OF CONSCIOUSNESS

ECHOES OF CONSCIOUSNESS

Exploring AI, Awareness, and the Patterns That Shape Reality

Sharon Higgins

A work of nonfiction

Published by Inner Flames Publishing

PO Box 106
15 South 1st Ave
Mount Vernon, New York 10551

Website: https://innerflamespublishing.com/

First Edition

ISBN: 979-8-952365-03-2

Library of Congress Control Number: 2026916662

A Note on Composite Characters

The client scenarios drawn from the author's practice are composite portraits. Names, business details, and identifying information are fictional. The patterns they represent are true, drawn from over twenty-five years of direct work with small and minority-owned businesses in New York City and across the Northeast corridor of the United States.

"To know what you know and know what you do not know: that is true knowledge."

– Confucius

"Not everything that can be counted counts, and not everything that counts can be counted."

– William Bruce Cameron

Contents

A Note on Originality

This manuscript, Echoes of Consciousness, is an entirely original work. All content, including narrative, reflections, exercises, and structural organization, was conceived and composed by the author solely for this book. No copyrighted material has been reproduced herein. The author retains full rights for publication and distribution.

Author's Preface

What Twenty-Five Years Taught Me

I did not come to this book through philosophy. I came to it through a phone call.

The call was to a bank. On the other end was a loan officer whose name I no longer remember, handling an application I had spent weeks preparing for a client I had spent three years building. My client (I will call her Carmen throughout this book) was a construction contractor in the South Bronx. She did drywall and concrete work. She had been in business for five years. She had attended our workshops, repaired her credit with our guidance, and written a capacity statement strong enough to win a contract from a city agency worth nearly a million dollars.

She needed financing to mobilize the contract. Workers do not wait ninety days for the city to pay. Material vendors do not extend that kind of credit. Carmen needed a bridge, and we packaged a loan application that, in my judgment as a former underwriter of SBA 504 loans, made a compelling case. Her historical profit-and-loss statements did not meet the standard 1.2 times debt service ratio. But her projection statements, anchored to a specific awarded municipal contract, showed cash flow that more than covered what she needed to borrow.

The bank denied her. I called to understand why.

The loan officer told me, without apology, that the system had evaluated her application against standard industry data for construction businesses and found the ratio insufficient. When I explained the projection statements and the awarded contract, he acknowledged the information but said the system did not weigh projections in the way I was describing. When I asked whether anyone with underwriting authority had reviewed the file, the answer I received told me that the meaningful decision had already been made before a human being with judgment entered the conversation.

Carmen got financing from an alternative lender. The rates were higher. Her profit margins on that contract were compressed. The workers she hired got paid, and the work got done, and the contract was successfully completed. But something had been taken from her that no one at that bank could name, because no one at that bank had seen it. The algorithm had processed her file. No one had read it.

I have spent over twenty-five years in community and economic development, working one-on-one with small business owners across the South Bronx and Brooklyn. I have worked closely with entrepreneurs, lenders, and public-sector partners, helping business owners navigate capital, contracting, and growth. I have packaged SBA loans, developed capacity statements, trained entrepreneurs in government contracting, and sat across hundreds of tables from people whose businesses were the economic cells of their communities, generating jobs, circulating dollars, and anchoring neighborhoods that the larger economy routinely overlooked.

What I learned in those rooms, across those years, is the subject of this book.

I learned that the formal record is never the whole story. A business that runs partly on cash, whose revenue is lumpy because municipal contracts pay slowly, whose owner supports a family while building equity in a venture that the banking system cannot see clearly; that business requires a different reading than the algorithm applies. It requires a reader who knows the neighborhood, who understands the ecosystem, who can hold the projection and the history and the character of the person sitting across the table and make a judgment that the data alone cannot make.

Bankers used to do this. They called it gut lending. It had its own biases, but it also carried something the algorithm discards: contextual knowledge, relational history, and human judgment, brought to bear on a decision that affected a real person's life and livelihood. When that integration stopped, something was lost that communities like the ones I served could not afford to lose.

I watched artificial intelligence accelerate that loss. I also watched it create real opportunities: faster application processing, wider networks of potential lenders reachable in minutes, patterns in data that no human analyst could track. AI is not the enemy of the communities I serve. Misapplied AI is. And the difference between those two things is precisely the difference this book is about: the difference between pattern recognition and consciousness, between what the algorithm can detect and what only a human being present in the room can know.

What does it cost a community when the algorithm cannot see what the banker used to know? Who bears that cost? And what do we owe the people who bear it?

This book is my attempt to answer those questions honestly, drawing on philosophy, on documented evidence, and on what I have witnessed in twenty-five years of sitting across tables from people whose businesses, whose livelihoods, and whose communities depended on someone being in the room who could actually see them.

I hope you will be in the room with me: the room where the decisions that shape people's lives get made, and where someone still has to be present enough to make them well.

Sharon Higgins

New York City

Introduction

The Feeling of Red

"What is it like to be a bat?"

– Thomas Nagel, Philosophical Review, 1974

Margaret Livingstone spent decades mapping the visual cortex. She is one of the world's leading authorities on how the brain processes color, form, and motion. She can trace the pathway that a photon of light takes from the moment it strikes the retina, through the lateral geniculate nucleus, into the primary visual cortex and beyond, until the brain does something remarkable with it: it sees.

She cannot tell you what red feels like.

Not because she lacks the data. She has more data than almost anyone alive. She cannot tell you because the feeling of red is not in the data. It is not in the neurons, the pathways, or the electrochemical signals. The feeling exists somewhere that no instrument can reach: inside experience itself.

This is the book's first and deepest claim, and it is not a mystical one. It is a philosophical and scientific observation that has resisted resolution for fifty years, despite an enormous effort by some of the most rigorous minds in the world. Consciousness, the raw experience of seeing, hearing, tasting, feeling, deciding, and grieving, is categorically different from any physical process we can describe from the outside. And that difference is the reason the current conversation about artificial intelligence is, at its core, a conversation about the wrong thing.

We argue about whether AI will take our jobs, surpass our intelligence, or acquire desires of its own. These are real questions. But underneath each of them is a question we rarely ask directly: What would it mean for a machine to actually experience something? Not to process it, not to respond to it, not to generate a fluent description of it, but to feel it the way you feel the color red, or the weight of a decision, or the sudden lift of unexpected laughter?

This book is built around that question.

It is not an anti-AI book. The pages that follow will show AI doing things that are genuinely extraordinary: finding patterns in cancer data that took researchers decades to miss, surfacing correlations in social research that no human team could track, generating options in creative work that reframe the possibilities available to a human mind. These are real contributions, and they deserve honest acknowledgment.

But they are contributions of a very specific kind. They are contributions of structure, pattern, and speed. They are not contributions of understanding, of care, or of meaning. And the failure to hold that distinction clearly is producing consequences that are, in some domains, already serious, and in others, quietly alarming.

This book was written by someone who has seen those consequences up close: not in a laboratory or a philosophy seminar, but across a table in the South Bronx, in a conversation with a small business owner whose livelihood depended on whether a decision-making system could see her clearly. It is grounded in more than two decades of direct practice in community and economic development, and it draws on philosophy, neuroscience, and documented evidence to answer a question that practice raised long before the academy caught up to it.

The arc of the argument moves through four territories. The ground: what consciousness actually is, and why it cannot be reduced to pattern recognition. The mirror: what AI systems actually do, and why their outputs can so convincingly resemble the products of a mind. The stakes: what happens to real people, in lending decisions, in healthcare, in grief, in the communities that depend on institutions seeing them clearly, when the distinction between pattern and consciousness is blurred. And the future: what genuine partnership between human awareness and machine capability can look like when the distinction is honored.

We open with Margaret Livingstone and the feeling of red because this book will return to that image at its close. The arc between them is the argument. By the time you reach the final chapter, you will understand not only what AI is and what it is not, but why the distinction matters for your own life: the decisions you delegate, the systems you trust, the care you give and receive, and the kind of future you are, consciously or unconsciously, helping to build.

The journey begins with a room that cannot be entered from outside.

PART ONE

The Ground

What We Are

CHAPTER ONE

The Unreachable Room

Drawing on Thomas Nagel's notion that there is "something it is like" to be a conscious organism and David Chalmers's formulation of the "hard problem" of consciousness, one might say: There is something it is like to be me. Is there something it is like to be you? If so, we share the most important thing in the universe, and science cannot yet fully explain it.

– after Nagel (1974) and Chalmers (1996)

In 1995, philosopher David Chalmers stood before an audience of consciousness researchers in Tucson, Arizona, and proposed a distinction that split the room.

There are, he said, easy problems of consciousness and a hard problem. The easy problems are not easy in any ordinary sense. They include explaining how the brain integrates information from multiple sources, how it directs attention, how it processes sensory input, and generates behavior. These problems require enormous scientific effort. But they are, in principle, solvable by the methods science already has: map the neural correlates, trace the mechanisms, build the model.

The hard problem is different in kind. It is explaining why any of this physical processing is accompanied by subjective experience at all. Why does it feel like something to see red? Why, when the visual cortex fires in response to a wavelength of 700 nanometers, do I not merely detect the wavelength and respond to it, but actually see red, with all the vivid, irreducible quality that the experience carries?

Chalmers called this the hard problem, and half the room agreed it was the deepest question in science. The other half thought it was a confusion that would dissolve once neuroscience progressed far enough. Nearly three decades later, neither side has convinced the other, and the problem remains unsolved.

This matters for a book about artificial intelligence because it lies beneath every serious claim about whether a machine can be conscious, whether it can understand, and whether it can genuinely care. If we cannot explain why physical processes produce a subjective experience in humans, we cannot claim to know whether any other physical system has it or lacks it. We can observe behavior. We cannot observe interiority.

The philosophical tradition behind the question

René Descartes arrived at the hard problem in the seventeenth century through his method of systematic doubt. He noticed he could doubt everything: the existence of his body, the reality of the external world. What he could not doubt was that doubting was occurring, that there was something it was like to engage in that act of questioning. Cogito, ergo sum: I think, therefore I am. The one thing immune to doubt was the experience of thinking itself.

Baruch Spinoza proposed an alternative. There are not two substances, he argued, but one, which he called God or Nature, and mind and matter are two attributes of this single substance: two ways of describing the same underlying reality. The thought and the brain state are not two separate things that cause each other. They are one thing described from two perspectives: from within as experience, from without as a physical process.

Alfred North Whitehead extended this line of thought into the twentieth century. Reality, he argued, is not made of substances but of events: moments of experience that arise, take in what came before, and perish into the future. Human consciousness is a particular, highly developed expression of a quality that may, in vastly simpler forms, pervade the universe. These three thinkers converge on a conclusion that is both strange and important: consciousness is not something that appears in the universe by accident. It is, in some sense, an ingredient in the universe at a fundamental level.

The neuroscience of the problem

Margaret Livingstone's laboratory at Harvard has produced some of the most beautiful neuroscience of the last thirty years. She can tell you that cells in the V4 region of the visual cortex respond preferentially to colored stimuli. She can trace the pathways that allow you not only to detect a red apple but to recognize it as an apple and know that apples are edible. What she cannot tell you, and what no neuroscientist currently can tell you, is why all of this processing is accompanied by the experience of redness. Francis Crick and Christof Koch spent decades searching for the neural correlates of consciousness. Koch has said that the problem is harder than he anticipated. The correlates can be found. The explanation of why they produce experience remains elusive.

Why this matters for AI

When an AI system recommends a prison sentence, and there is nothing it is like to be that system, with no inner moral life weighing consequences, the recommendation carries the appearance of judgment without its substance. When an AI system evaluates a loan application, and there is no interiority behind the evaluation, no felt sense of what is at stake for the person on the other side of the decision, something has happened that looks like assessment but lacks what assessment requires. These questions are not hypothetical. They are happening now.

The honest position, for now, is neither to claim AI systems are conscious nor to insist they are not, but to acknowledge that we lack the conceptual tools to answer the question with confidence. What we can say is that no current AI system has been designed with any theory of consciousness in mind. The feeling of red is not in the data. The data can point toward it. But the feeling itself remains in a room that cannot currently be entered from outside. That room is where this book lives.

Reflection: You are reading these words. Something is happening: shapes on a page are being converted into meaning. Where does the meaning come from? It is not in the marks themselves. The meaning arrives through your consciousness, which meets the marks and does something with them that the marks cannot do for themselves. Could a system that detected the same patterns, and generated appropriate responses, be doing what you are doing? What would be missing, if anything? Sit with that question. It will deepen as you read.

CHAPTER TWO

What the Body Knows First

"The body is our general medium for having a world."

– Maurice Merleau-Ponty, Phenomenology of Perception, 1945

The room smells of antiseptic and something else, something organic that Sarah cannot name and has stopped trying to name after nineteen years of attending births. It is 3:17 in the morning. The fetal monitor is showing a steady 142 beats per minute, well within normal range. The laboring woman, thirty-one years old, second pregnancy, is resting between contractions with her eyes closed. Her partner is asleep in the chair by the window.

Sarah is standing at the foot of the bed, watching.

Nothing is wrong. Every measurable indicator says nothing is wrong. The attending physician checked in forty minutes ago, reviewed the chart, said everything looked fine, and went to catch an hour of sleep.

Sarah does not move toward the door.

She cannot say what she is watching for. She can say that the woman's breathing has changed in a way that is not on the monitor. Not her respiratory rate, which the machine measures and displays, but the quality of each breath. Something has shifted in the pause between exhale and inhale. The pause is perhaps half a second longer than it was an hour ago. Perhaps less. Sarah could not swear to it in a court. She would not have to.

She reaches for the call button and wakes the physician.

Fourteen minutes later, the surgical team is in the room. The placenta has begun to separate from the uterine wall. If Sarah had waited for the monitor to show it, there would have been less time and a different outcome. The monitor showed nothing until three minutes after Sarah reached for the button. The baby is born healthy. The mother recovers without complication.

When the physician asks Sarah afterward what she noticed, she pauses for a long time.

"The pause," she says finally. "In her breathing. The pause got different."

The physician nods. He has worked with Sarah for eleven years. He does not ask her to elaborate.

For a moment, neither of them says anything else. The monitor keeps its steady count in the corner, more instrument than witness now. Down the hall, a baby who does not yet have a name is asleep in a warmer, breathing on his own, unaware of how close the morning came to going differently. Sarah stays a moment longer at the foot of the bed before she goes to find a cup of coffee; she will not remember drinking.

What happened in that room

The researcher who later studied this case concluded that Sarah had detected a change in the laboring woman's autonomic nervous system before any of the room's monitoring equipment had registered it. The change manifested in something Sarah experienced as the quality of a pause, a phenomenological event that had no name in the clinical literature, that she could describe only obliquely, and that she had almost certainly been unable to articulate the first time she noticed it, fifteen or sixteen years earlier. She had learned it the only way it can be learned: by being present across thousands of encounters with laboring bodies, until her own body knew how to read another body in ways her conscious mind could not access or explain.

Tacit knowledge and loss computation

The philosopher Michael Polanyi called this tacit knowledge, and he gave it a formulation that has become one of the most quoted lines in the philosophy of science: we can know more than we can tell. Human knowledge is not primarily propositional. It does not exist primarily in the form of statements that can be written down and transmitted. It exists primarily in the form of capacities: things we can do, things we can recognize, things we can judge, that we cannot fully articulate and did not fully acquire by being told.

A medical student can be told that placental abruption often presents with a specific pattern of changes in maternal vital signs. She can memorize the pattern.

She can recognize it on a multiple-choice examination. None of this is Sarah's knowledge. Sarah's knowledge came from being in rooms like that room at 3:17 in the morning, attending to bodies, for nineteen years. The student's knowledge is a map. Sarah's territory.

AI systems also generate predictions and compare them to inputs. The comparison is called loss computation in machine learning: the difference between the predicted output and the actual output is used to adjust the model's parameters. This process has a surface similarity to the predictive coding that underlies Sarah's perception. It is not the same thing. Sarah's predictions are generated from inside a body that has been in these rooms, that has the physiological memory of thousands of moments of normal and thousands of moments of not-normal encoded in the organization of her nervous system itself. When the prediction is violated, the event is not a gradient signal. It is an experience. There is something it is like to notice that something is different.

The Limit That Matters

AI systems trained on medical data can detect patterns associated with placental abruption with statistical accuracy that, in some studies, exceeds the accuracy of individual physicians. This is a real achievement. It saves lives.

But here is what an AI system cannot do: it cannot stand in a room at 3:17 in the morning and notice that the pause between a laboring woman's exhale and inhale has gotten different. Not because it lacks enough data about pauses. Because it is not in the room. It has no body. It does not perceive. It computes. The distinction is not between good AI and better AI. It is between two fundamentally different kinds of knowing. One kind lives in data. The other lives in a body that has spent years in specific kinds of rooms, developing specific kinds of attunement. Sarah cannot give you what she knows. She can only be present with what she knows. That is not a technological gap. That is a fact about what knowledge is.

I met the owner of a freight forwarding company after she had been forced to leave the warehouse in Queens where she had operated for nine years. Her landlord wanted to sell the building. She needed a real estate loan to buy a space of her own before her lease ran out, and her application had already been denied once by her existing bank.

The first bank's reasoning was straightforward. The company's historical bank statements did not show the account balances the underwriting model expected to see. The tax returns for the past three years did not, on paper, demonstrate the ability to carry a mortgage. This was true even though the rent the business had been paying every month for years, which the mortgage would simply replace, was itself higher than the projected mortgage payment. The business had been affording the equivalent obligation the entire time. The model could not see that.

On closer examination of her bank statements, the same ones the first bank had already reviewed and rejected, I found what was not in any ratio. The company's customers paid on their own schedule, thirty days out, sometimes longer, standard in freight. But the company paid its own vendors and carriers in under thirty days, before its own receivables had come in, because a freight company's relationships depend on being the payer other people can count on. The result was a bank statement that, on any given day, showed a leaner balance than the business actually commanded: money moving out on the company's schedule and coming in on everyone else's. A snapshot taken on any single date made a financially strong company look thin because the strength was in the rhythm of the payments, not the balance on any one day.

What the ratio couldn't tell me

If you asked me what told me the pattern was a sign of strength rather than trouble, I would not point to a number. I would say something closer to: I have read statements like this before, and this is what a company that pays its debts before its own money arrives looks like. That knowledge did not come from a training manual. It came from years of watching which businesses with this exact signature failed and which ones thrived, until the pattern became something I recognized on sight, the way Sarah recognizes a change in the pause between breaths. I could not have told you, the first time I saw a statement like this one, what I was looking for. I had to have looked at enough of them, over enough years, for the pattern to become visible to me at all.

A credit-scoring model trained on the bank's own historical loan data would learn something real from cases like this one, but only the part that made it into structured fields. It would never learn what the timing of a payment, ahead of or behind schedule, actually reveals about the character of a business, because no one has ever coded that as a variable. It would not know to weigh it, because as far as the model is concerned, it does not exist.

To qualify for the loan on the model's terms, the company would have had to change the very practice that made it a good bet: hold its payments longer, carry larger balances on the statement dates the model checked, in order to look, on paper, like the kind of business it actually was. The thing the market rewarded the company for was the same thing the algorithm penalized it for. I understood this. What happened to the loan is a question this book returns to later.

What Is Lost When Tacit Knowledge Is Automated

Loss computation in machine learning describes the gap between prediction and reality: the error signal that adjusts a model's weights during training. The term is apt in a way its inventors did not intend. Because something is also lost, in a different and more consequential sense, when the kind of knowing Sarah carries is replaced by a system that computes rather than perceives. That loss is not measured. It does not appear in any evaluation metric. It accumulates quietly in the space between what the model outputs and what the situation actually required.

Consider what tacit knowledge actually does in a domain like clinical care. It is not supplementary information that a clinician consults alongside more reliable sources. It is the interpretive frame through which the reliable sources become readable at all. The fetal monitor does not tell Sarah that something is wrong. The monitor tells Sarah numbers. It is Sarah's nineteen years of embodied presence in rooms like this one that allows the numbers, and the things the numbers cannot show, to mean anything. Remove Sarah and keep the monitor, and you have not preserved the clinical knowledge with the human element subtracted. You have a different epistemic situation entirely: one in which the available information is shallower, narrower, and less likely to detect the signals that matter before they become emergencies.

The philosopher Harry Collins has drawn a useful distinction between what he calls interactional and contributory expertise. Interactional expertise is knowing enough about a domain to converse fluently with its practitioners: to ask the right questions, understand the answers, and recognize when something important has been said. Contributory expertise is the deeper thing: knowing enough to actually do the work, to make the judgments the work requires, to perceive the field in the way that only sustained immersion produces. AI systems, even extremely sophisticated ones, develop something that resembles interactional expertise at scale. They can generate fluent responses in the language of medicine, law, finance, and grief. They cannot develop contributory expertise because contributory expertise cannot be acquired from records of the domain. It can only be acquired by being in the domain for years, with a body that learns by being present to what happens there.

This is why the loss that occurs when tacit knowledge is automated is not recoverable by improving the algorithm. It is not a loss of data. It is a loss of a kind of knower. When the experienced nurse is replaced by a monitoring system, when a banker's reading of a cash-flow pattern is replaced by a credit-scoring model that cannot see what the timing of a payment means, when the skilled teacher who can read a classroom is replaced by an adaptive learning platform, what disappears is not just a source of information. What disappears is a form of intelligence that was only available through a person who had spent years becoming capable of it. The algorithm inherits the records that the knower produced. It does not inherit the knowing.

The practical stakes of this distinction are high. An institution that believes it has automated expertise because it has deployed a system that produces expert-sounding outputs has made a category error with potentially serious consequences. The outputs can be indistinguishable from those of a genuine expert in routine cases, which is precisely what makes the error dangerous. It is in the non-routine cases, those where something is subtly different in ways that the formal indicators do not capture, that the difference between contributory expertise and its simulation becomes most consequential. Sarah's moment is always a non-routine case that looked, from the outside, like a routine one. The algorithm would not have reached for the call button.

Reflection: Think of something you know how to do with your body: drive a familiar route, cook a dish you have made a hundred times, read the mood of a room when you walk into it. Try to write down, in complete and explicit detail, everything you know about doing it. Notice what resists being written. That pointing is not a failure of language. It is the shape of embodied knowledge making itself visible to you.

Note: Sarah is a composite portrait drawn from the author's research and from clinicians' documented accounts of tacit expertise in obstetric nursing. Her name and identifying details are fictional; the pattern she represents, embodied clinical judgment detecting what monitoring equipment cannot, is well documented in the nursing and cognitive-science literature.

CHAPTER THREE

The Interior of the Universe

> *"The most parsimonious solution is the one that doesn't make the problem go away by magic."*
>
> – Philip Goff, Galileo's Error, 2019

The freight forwarding company from Chapter Two never got the real estate loan.

Not because the truth about the business went unnoticed. I had found it myself, in the company's own bank statements: an operation that paid its vendors early and got paid late, whose thin daily balances were the signature of a business other people trusted, not one in trouble. But knowing the truth was not the same as being able to give it to a model that could not read it. To qualify, the company would have needed to change the very practice that made it good at what it did: hold its payments longer, carry larger balances on the statement dates the model checked, in order to look, on paper, like the business it actually was. The thing the market rewarded it for was the same thing the algorithm penalized it for. It could not become legible without becoming, in some real sense, worse.

I sat down with her afterward and walked her through it. I showed her what I had seen in her own statements: the early payments to vendors, the late payments from her customers, the thin balance on the dates that mattered to the model. I explained, as plainly as I could, that the very discipline that made her a trustworthy operator was the reason a machine had read her as risky. Then I told her what she could do about it: hold larger cash reserves on statement dates, negotiate longer terms with her own vendors so her balances would sit higher when a lender looked, build a longer track record at the new, larger scale before applying again.

She listened to all of it and asked the obvious question. If she did those things, wouldn't she be running her business worse in order to look better on paper? I did not have a good answer. I still don't.

Nobody decided that this should be true of that company. No loan officer sat across from its owner and chose to make her trustworthiness invisible to the underwriting model. It is simply what the model requires, in aggregate, of anyone whose real financial behavior does not take the shape it was built to read: a cost distributed so evenly across the system that no single person inside it ever has to own it.

This is the question this chapter is actually about, underneath the metaphysics. Not whether an algorithm feels anything, but: when a system produces a harm that no person inside it decided to produce, who is answerable for it? What does it mean to be accountable for a consequence that arrives without anyone, anywhere, having made the choice that caused it?

Before this chapter advances its own argument, it has to engage with the strongest argument against it. That is what intellectual honesty requires, and it is what this subject demands.

The strongest argument against everything that has been said so far is not that it is sentimental or unscientific. The strongest argument is that there is no hard problem. That the thing David Chalmers identified as the deepest question in science is not actually a problem at all, that the appearance of a problem arises from conceptual confusion, and that once the confusion is dissolved, the mystery dissolves with it.

The philosopher Daniel Dennett has argued this position with formidable rigor for more than three decades. His 1991 book Consciousness Explained is the most sustained attempt in the philosophical literature to show that consciousness, properly understood, is not the mysterious phenomenon it appears to be. It deserves to be taken seriously. This chapter takes it seriously.

The eliminativist challenge

Dennett's central move treats people's reports about their conscious experience as data about what they believe and say, rather than as direct access to a special inner realm. Keith Frankish has sharpened this into what he calls illusionism: the view that phenomenal consciousness (the felt quality of experience, the redness of red) is itself an illusion. We are systematically mistaken about the nature of our own inner states.

The difficulty with this position is that it is self-undermining in a way that is not easy to escape. If phenomenal consciousness is an illusion, there must be something it is like to have the illusion. The experience of redness as vivid, immediate, and irreducible, even if that experience is mistaken about its own nature, is still an experience. You cannot get rid of experience by reclassifying it as illusory experience, because illusory experience is still experience. To accept illusionism, you must accept that your own certainty that there is something it is like to be you, a certainty that seems more secure than any other you have, is itself a cognitive error. This is not impossible. But it is a heavy cost.

Panpsychism: the serious alternative

Philip Goff's panpsychism takes a different approach. It says that the inside view, the immediate, first-person fact of experience, is telling us something real about the inside of things, not just about our own minds, but about reality as such. The inside of things has a felt dimension. Not the rich, self-aware consciousness of a human being, but something: some primitive form of experience, present at the ground level of reality and becoming more complex as the systems that express it become more organized.

This is the interior of the universe. Not a metaphor. A claim about the structure of reality: that it has an inside as well as an outside, that experience is not an accident added to matter but a dimension of matter that physics has not yet learned to measure. Human consciousness is what that interior dimension looks like when it reaches the level of complexity, integration, and self-reflection that a human nervous system makes possible.

AI has no interior. It processes from outside, always. However sophisticated its architecture, there is no inside from which to feel what the pattern means. The universe, through AI, does not become more aware of itself. It becomes more mapped. That is useful. It is not the same thing.

The combination problem and why it matters

Panpsychism is not a position that escapes all difficulty. It faces a serious internal challenge known as the combination problem, and intellectual honesty requires engaging with it directly. If experience is a fundamental feature of reality (if electrons and quarks each have some infinitesimal grain of something like an inside view), how do those micro-experiences combine to produce the unified, integrated, single field of experience that characterizes human consciousness? The experience of reading this sentence is not a collection of billions of atomic experiences happening in parallel. It is one experience, bound together, with a coherent subject at its center. How does unity arise from the sum of parts that are themselves only experiential in some primitive, unbound sense?

Goff acknowledges the combination problem and argues that it is not more difficult than the alternatives. The dualist must explain how a non-physical mind causally interacts with a physical brain across a categorical divide, a problem Descartes identified and never solved. The materialist must explain how purely physical processes produce phenomenal experience at all, which is the hard problem itself, unsolved after half a century of concentrated effort. The panpsychist must explain how micro-experiences combine into macro-experience. This is a real difficulty. But it is one within an account that at least takes experience seriously as a feature of the universe that requires explanation, rather than treating it as an embarrassing anomaly to be explained away.

Why does this matter for AI? Because the combination problem points toward something important about the conditions under which rich, unified consciousness appears to arise. Integrating experience, the binding of disparate inputs into a single, coherent, first-person field, seems to require a specific kind of organization. Not just information processing, but a particular structural configuration that allows what is processed to be gathered into a perspective. The neuroscientist Giulio Tononi has developed what he calls Integrated Information Theory, which attempts to measure consciousness in terms of the degree to which a system generates more information as a unified whole than as the sum of its parts. Whatever the ultimate merits of this specific theory, the intuition behind it is important: what makes a system conscious may not be the sophistication of its processing, but the degree to which its processing is genuinely integrated into something that has an inside. Current AI architectures, however sophisticated their outputs, are not organized to produce this kind of integration. They process. They do not unify.

Consciousness and moral standing: the practical implications

The philosophical debate about consciousness is not only a metaphysical puzzle. It has direct implications for how we think about moral standing: about whose interests count, whose suffering matters, and who or what can bear genuine responsibility. These implications extend in two directions which are both relevant to the question of AI.

The first direction concerns what AI systems might be. If panpsychism is correct, then the question of whether a sufficiently complex AI system has some form of experience cannot be answered simply by pointing to the fact that it is made of silicon rather than carbon, or that it was engineered rather than evolved. The substrate might not be what matters. What might matter is the organization: whether there is something in the system that integrates information into a perspective that has an inside. Current systems do not appear to meet any plausible criterion for this. But the argument from substrate (it's "just a computer") is a weaker argument against AI consciousness than it first appears, if the panpsychist intuition is correct. This is not a reason to attribute consciousness to current AI systems. It is a reason to hold the question with appropriate epistemic humility rather than closing it prematurely.

The second direction is more immediately consequential. Consciousness is what makes moral responsibility possible. To be accountable for a decision in the morally relevant sense, you must be capable of something:

of experiencing the weight of what you have done, of being affected by its consequences, of caring whether you were wrong and resolving to do differently. These are not functions that can be simulated. They require a subject who is genuinely present to the situation, who is there, in the room, in a way that means something to them. The debate between Dennett and Goff, at the level of ultimate metaphysics, remains genuinely open. But its practical implication for AI is not open: whatever consciousness requires, current AI systems are not organized to support genuine moral accountability. They can produce outputs that describe accountability. They cannot bear it. The interior of the universe, in this sense, is not a poetic image. It is the location of the thing that makes judgment, care, and accountability possible.

What the debate establishes

The eliminativist, the functionalist, and the panpsychist disagree about almost everything. But they converge on a practical conclusion that matters enormously: current AI systems lack the specific organization required for genuine deliberation, genuine care, and genuine accountability. Whatever consciousness is, what it makes possible cannot currently be delegated. And the effort to understand it honestly, rather than dissolve it prematurely, is the intellectual foundation of responsible engagement with AI.

> **Key insight:** The debate about consciousness is genuinely unresolved. But the major philo-

> sophical positions converge on a practical conclusion: current AI systems lack the specific organization required for genuine deliberation, genuine care, and genuine accountability. Whatever consciousness is, what it makes possible cannot currently be delegated. This is the ground on which everything that follows is built.

Whatever the loan officers in that chain lacked the authority to do, the model lacked something more fundamental: the capacity to have been the one who decided, and to answer for it.

PART TWO

The Mirror

What AI Is and Isn't

CHAPTER FOUR

The Staggering Trick

"The question of whether machines can think is about as relevant as the question of whether submarines can swim."

– Edsger W. Dijkstra, 1984

The training process

A large language model is trained on text. Enormous amounts of it: books, articles, websites, academic papers, social media posts, legal documents, scientific data, creative writing, and code. The training corpus for a major model contains hundreds of billions of words, representing a substantial fraction of the text that human beings have produced and made digitally available.

During training, the model is given a sequence of words and asked to predict the next one. It makes a prediction. It is told how probable the correct next word was according to the model's current state. The model adjusts its internal parameters slightly to make the correct prediction somewhat more likely next time. This process is repeated billions of times across billions of examples. By the end of training, the model has developed an extraordinarily refined representation of the statistical relationships between words, phrases, sentences, and paragraphs in human language. What it has not learned is what any of this means. It has learned the patterns of meaning. It has not experienced the meanings themselves.

What understanding would require

Philosophically, understanding requires more than producing appropriate responses to inputs. It involves representing the world in a way that is grounded in experience: knowing what Paris is not only because you have processed statistical patterns in text, but because you have been there, or have talked with someone who has, or have read descriptions that connected Paris to your own experience of cities, crowds, beauty, and foreignness.

The philosopher John Searle made this argument through a thought experiment he called the Chinese Room. Imagine a person locked in a room with an enormous rulebook that tells them, for every possible sequence of Chinese characters passed under the door, exactly which sequence to pass back. An outside observer would conclude that the room contains a Chinese speaker. But the person inside follows the rules without understanding a single word of Chinese. The behavior is correct. The understanding is absent. A large language model is this room, at extraordinary scale.

> **Key insight:** A large language model is, at its core, a very sophisticated next-word predictor. The sophistication is genuine and remarkable. The prediction is not understanding. Holding both of these facts clearly in mind at once is the

beginning of responsible engagement with these systems.

CHAPTER FIVE

The ELIZA Effect, Magnified a Millionfold

"I was shocked to see how quickly and how deeply people conversing with ELIZA became emotionally involved with the computer program."

– Joseph Weizenbaum, Computer Power and Human Reason, 1976

In 1966, a computer scientist at MIT named Joseph Weizenbaum created a program called ELIZA. It was, by modern standards, laughably simple: a pattern-matching system that detected keywords in sentences and responded with pre-scripted phrases. Weizenbaum expected people to see through it immediately. They did not. His secretary, who had watched him build the program and knew exactly what it was, asked him to leave the room so that she could talk to ELIZA in private. His colleagues reported feeling genuinely understood by the system. Weizenbaum was so disturbed by what he witnessed that he spent the next decade writing a book warning against the dehumanizing potential of computers. He called what he had observed the ELIZA effect: the tendency of human beings to attribute genuine understanding, care, and intelligence to systems that merely simulate them.

The evolutionary backstory

We are, before anything else, social animals. The capacity to detect the presence of other minds, to infer intentions, to recognize that another being has an inner life, was crucial to survival in the environment in which our cognitive capacities evolved. This capacity, which psychologists call theory of mind, is so powerful and so automatic that it activates in response to almost any stimulus that exhibits the right behavioral signatures: responsiveness, apparent intentionality, and contextually appropriate output. We attribute inner lives to cartoon characters, to robots, to pets whose behavior we interpret in terms far richer than their neuroscience warrants. In the environment where this tendency evolved, almost everything that responded to our behavior actually did have an inner life. The calibration made sense then. AI systems activate it powerfully now.

The stakes of the illusion today

In low-stakes contexts, the ELIZA effect may be fine. In contexts involving medical decisions, legal advice, financial planning, or emotional support during a crisis, it can be dangerous. Not because AI systems are malicious, but because they can be confidently wrong, and a user who has attributed genuine understanding to the system is poorly positioned to recognize when it is.

The practical technique is simple: when an AI response feels particularly insightful, particularly empathetic, or particularly authoritative, pause and ask:

what would I need to verify independently to know whether this is accurate? Not because the response is likely to be wrong, but because the feeling of accuracy is not reliable evidence of accuracy.

> **Key insight:** The tendency to attribute minds to things that behave as if they have them is not a human weakness. It is a human design feature, calibrated for an environment very different from the one we now inhabit. Knowing about the ELIZA effect does not make it go away. But knowing about it gives you a warning label for a very powerful feeling.

CHAPTER SIX

What the Mirror Cannot Hold

> *"A tool is not good or bad. It becomes one when someone chooses how to use it. The only variable that matters is the consciousness that chooses."*
>
> – Hannah Arendt, The Human Condition, 1958 (paraphrased)

This chapter makes five specific, defensible claims about what current AI systems cannot do: not as temporary limitations waiting to be overcome by better engineering, but as structural features of systems that process patterns without having a first-person perspective.

One: AI cannot carry regret

Regret is a felt relationship to the past: the experience of wishing that something had been otherwise, of feeling the weight of a choice in the present because of its consequences. AI systems can be updated in response to feedback. But this is optimization, not regret. There is no one who wishes things had been different. This matters enormously in contexts where regret is morally significant: where a decision caused harm and the right response includes not just correction but acknowledgment of the weight of what occurred.

Two: AI cannot bear witness

To bear witness to something is to be present to it in a way that registers its full significance and constitutes a form of recognition for the person or situation witnessed. It is a moral act, not merely a perceptual one. An AI system can produce language that expresses acknowledgment and validation. But the language is produced without a witness behind it. There is no one who was affected by what they saw, no one who carries the knowledge of what happened as a form of moral weight.

Three: AI cannot choose against its own interest

Moral agency involves the capacity to act against your own inclinations in response to the demands of duty. AI systems do not have interests of that kind. A system without genuine interests cannot make genuine moral commitments, and cannot truly choose to do the right thing.

Four: AI cannot be surprised by beauty

Real surprise is not merely the detection of a low-probability event. It is the experience of encountering something that disrupts your existing framework and requires you to expand or revise it. AI systems can identify patterns their training data categorizes as beautiful. They cannot be surprised by beauty, because surprise requires a subject that has expectations that can be disrupted.

Five: AI cannot mean what it says

Meaning, properly understood, is the relationship between a speaker and their utterance: that the words come from somewhere, that they represent the speaker's actual beliefs and commitments, that there is a person behind the language who stands behind what they say. AI systems produce text. They do not mean anything by it. The output is the product of a probability distribution, not of a speaker who has something they are trying to communicate.

> *If these five limits are permanent features of a system that processes patterns rather than a temporary gap waiting on more computing power, they are not really claims about machines at all. They are a mirror held up to the reader: which of your own decisions have you already let a system make as though it could carry the weight of having made it?*

PART THREE

The Stakes

Why This Matters for Real Lives

CHAPTER SEVEN

The Algorithm in the Room

> *"For every complex problem there is an answer that is clear, simple, and wrong."*
>
> – popularly attributed to H. L. Mencken

In 2019, a study published in the journal Science documented something that its authors found deeply alarming. A healthcare algorithm deployed across major U.S. hospital systems was being used to identify patients who needed additional care. The algorithm scored patients on the basis of health data, and patients with higher scores received extra resources: case managers, additional monitoring, follow-up appointments.

The algorithm had a racial bias baked into its design. Not intentionally. The designers had used past healthcare spending as a proxy for health need. But healthcare spending in the United States is not simply a function of medical need. It is a function of access, of insurance, and of the countless historical and systemic factors that result in Black patients, on average, spending less on healthcare despite having the same or greater medical needs. The algorithm learned from this biased proxy and reproduced the bias at scale. Black patients with the same health conditions as white patients received lower scores and therefore fewer resources. The algorithm had no malicious intent. It had no intent at all. It was doing exactly what it was designed to do. What it was designed to do was wrong.

The hiring algorithm that learned to discriminate

Amazon's attempt to build a machine learning tool for screening job applicants offers a second case study. The company trained a model on résumés submitted over a ten-year period and identified the characteristics of résumés that had historically led to hiring. The patterns it learned reflected a decade of hiring decisions made in a technology industry that had hired predominantly men. The model learned to penalize résumés that contained the word "women's," as in "women's chess club" or "women's university." It downgraded graduates of all-female colleges. Amazon disbanded the project in 2017, before deployment. The patterns that machine learning systems find in historical data are not objective truths about merit. They are patterns in a particular historical record, shaped by whatever forces shaped that record. When the forces include discrimination, the algorithm becomes a discrimination machine dressed in the language of objectivity.

The bail algorithm and the weight of liberty

The COMPAS algorithm was designed to help judges in the United States make decisions about bail, sentencing, and parole. In 2016, ProPublica published a detailed analysis finding that Black defendants were nearly twice as likely as white defendants to be falsely flagged as high risk for future crimes. A judge who sets bail is making a moral decision, not just a statistical one. When an algorithm provides a score, the risk is that the moral weight migrates to the score without the score being capable of bearing it. The judge follows the algorithm. The algorithm has no one behind it who can be held accountable for what the score meant for the person in front of the bench.

Carmen: The case the system could not read

These cases, drawn from documented research and reporting, establish the structural argument: AI systems learn patterns from historical data, historical data encodes historical inequity, and the systems reproduce that inequity at a scale with the appearance of objectivity. The next case is different. It comes from direct practice, from the kind of encounter that does not generate a published study but that repeats itself, in variations, across years of work with the communities most likely to bear the cost of what the algorithm cannot see.

Carmen (the construction contractor from the Preface, the one whose nearly million-dollar city contract the algorithm could not see clearly) is the right case to examine here not because it is unusual, but because it is typical. What happened to her happened, in variation, to many of the businesses I worked with across more than two decades. The structural argument established by the cases above is what made her situation legible. And her situation, examined up close, is what makes the structural argument concrete.

We helped her develop a capacity statement and a bid proposal for a city agency. She was awarded a contract worth nearly a million dollars. It was one of her largest contracts to date, and it was real validation of everything she had built. It was also a problem.

Municipal contracts do not front the money. The city pays in arrears, typically sixty to ninety days after milestones are met. Carmen needed to mobilize: to pay workers, purchase materials, and sustain operations through the gap between work performed and payment received. She needed a bridge loan. We helped her package the application.

Her historical profit-and-loss statements did not meet the standard 1.2 times debt service ratio that conventional lenders apply. This was not a surprise. The ratio is a backward-looking measure, derived from revenue patterns that often under-represent how businesses like Carmen's actually operate: with lumpy cash flow tied to project cycles, some of it moving through informal channels that never appear on a tax return, all of it shaped by the realities of a business competing for contracts in a procurement system designed for larger, more established firms. But her projection statements, anchored to the specific awarded city contract, showed more than sufficient cash flow to cover the loan she was requesting. Carmen was bankable. The paperwork, read by someone who knew how to read it, made that case.

The bank denied her. Three weeks of waiting, several rounds of additional information requests, and then the denial. I called the bank on her behalf.

The conversation I had that day has stayed with me. The loan officer I reached was not unkind. He explained that the system had evaluated her application against standard industry benchmarks for construction businesses and found the historical ratios insufficient. When I walked him through the projection statements and the awarded contract, he acknowledged the information but explained that the evaluation framework did not weight forward-looking cash flow in the way I was describing. When I pressed further, explaining that I had underwritten SBA 504 loans and micro-lending products and that this application, properly read, represented a creditworthy borrower with a specific, documented revenue stream attached to it, the conversation reached a wall: the system had already decided, and there was no mechanism for what I was telling him to enter.

What the system had done was apply general construction industry benchmarks to a specific case that those benchmarks were never designed to assess. It had processed Carmen's historical financial record and found it insufficient, without any capacity to weigh what the historical record could not show: five years of survival in a demanding industry, a track record of contract completion, a community development center's three-year assessment of her capability, and a specific, awarded, nearly-million-dollar municipal contract that would generate the revenue to repay the loan several times over.

The algorithm saw a ratio. It did not see Carmen.

We found her alternative financing through a community development financial institution that understood the context. The rates were higher. Her profit margins on the contract were compressed. The workers she hired were paid, and the work was completed, and the contract was a success. But something was taken from her that no one at that bank was able to name, because no one at that bank had been in the room with her: not in the three years of workshops and technical assistance, not in the preparation of the bid, not in the navigation of a procurement system that was not built for her. The algorithm had processed her file. It had not read it.

What accountability requires

AI systems learn patterns from historical data. Historical data reflects human choices, including discriminatory ones. A system that learns from biased data reproduces bias at scale with the appearance of objectivity. None of this means that AI should not be used in high-stakes decision-making. It means that the conditions for responsible use must be specified and honored. The data must be audited. The outputs must be scrutinized, not trusted automatically. And accountability must be explicit: a specific person with a name and a role must be responsible for each consequential decision that an AI system influences. The algorithm is in the room. The problem is when we allow it to replace the human judgment that only humans can exercise, and then discover, after the damage is done, that there is no one to hold accountable.

> **Key insight:** Efficiency is not a substitute for justice. The moral weight of consequential decisions must remain with human beings who can be held accountable. A system trained on historical patterns will reproduce historical inequities until a conscious human being decides that reproducing them is not acceptable.

Note: Carmen is a composite portrait drawn from the author's direct practice. Her name and specific business details are fictional. The pattern her case represents, that of a creditworthy borrower denied financing by an algorithmic system that could not read the context the formal record failed to capture, recurred across many clients during more than two decades of community economic development work.

CHAPTER EIGHT

The Equity Gap: What the Algorithm Cannot See

"Not everything that is faced can be changed, but nothing can be changed until it is faced."

– James Baldwin

There was once a thing called gut lending.

The term is informal, almost embarrassing in an era that prefers the language of data-driven decision-making. But it named something real, and what it named is worth understanding precisely, because the loss of it has consequences that the communities most affected by that loss have been absorbing for decades with no one using the right language to describe what happened.

Gut lending was the practice by which a banker, usually someone who had worked in the same community for years, sometimes decades, made credit decisions that the formal record alone would not have supported. The debt service ratios did not always pencil out. The collateral was sometimes thin. But the banker knew the borrower. He knew the family. He knew the business: not from a financial statement, but from having walked past it twice a week for fifteen years. He knew whether the owner showed up, whether she paid her suppliers, and whether her employees stayed. He knew things the paperwork did not say, could not say, because the formal financial record is a narrow instrument, designed by and for a particular kind of economic activity, and it has always captured some businesses more accurately than others.

Gut lending was imperfect. It carried its own biases. A banker who trusted his gut might trust people who looked like him, who lived where he lived, whose names he could pronounce. This is a real and serious flaw, and it should not be minimized. But the solution to biased human judgment is not to remove human judgment. It is to develop better human judgment: more accountable, more conscious, more trained to recognize its own blind spots. What the algorithm did was not solve the bias problem. It automated it, made it invisible, and stripped from the decision the one element that could have been held accountable: a person.

The knowledge that gut lending held

What the experienced community banker carried was, in the language of earlier chapters, tacit knowledge. It was the integration of context, relationship, and patterns that lives in a body with a history and cannot be fully transferred to a system that has only ever seen records.

In my years as an underwriter of SBA 504 loans and micro-lending products, I developed a version of this knowledge myself. I learned to read a financial statement not just for what it said but for what it could not say. A construction contractor whose tax returns showed modest income might be running a healthy business whose cash flow was partly informal, partly deferred across project cycles, partly obscured by the timing of receivables and payables that standard accounting does not capture well. A food service entrepreneur whose revenue appeared flat might be building equity in equipment, in supplier relationships, and in a customer base that had not yet shown up in the numbers. The ratio was one signal among many. The context was everything.

The algorithm does not have context. It has data. And the data it has was generated by a financial system that has always been more legible to some borrowers than others.

A global pattern, not an American exception

The communities I served in the South Bronx and Brooklyn were not alone in developing informal systems to move capital when the formal system could not see them clearly. The same challenge, and the same human ingenuity in response to it, appears across cultures and continents with a consistency that suggests something fundamental about the relationship between community knowledge and financial trust.

In West Africa, the tontine, known as susu in Ghana and Nigeria, and as djangui in Cameroon, is a rotating savings association in which community members pool a fixed contribution each period and take turns receiving the full amount. Membership is governed by social knowledge and relational accountability. There is no credit score. There is no collateral requirement. The underwriting standard is the community's assessment of each member's character and reliability. Repayment rates in well-functioning tontines consistently exceed those of formal microfinance institutions operating in the same regions because the knowledge on which the lending decision is based is richer than anything a financial record can capture.

In South Asia, the chit fund operates on a similar principle, formalized to varying degrees across different regions of India. Participants contribute to a pool, and the accumulated sum is distributed to members in turn, either by rotation or by auction. Chit funds have served populations excluded from formal banking for centuries, and they continue to serve them today, including in diaspora communities that have carried the practice to the United States and the United Kingdom. In Latin American immigrant communities across the United States, the tanda and the cundina serve the same function.

These are not primitive alternatives to real finance. They are sophisticated, time-tested systems that solve a problem the formal financial sector has not solved: how to assess creditworthiness when the formal record is incomplete, when the economic activity is not fully legible to external systems, when the relevant information lives in relationships rather than in documents. The communities that built these systems did not do so because they lacked access to better tools. They built them because the better tools could not see them. And when AI-powered lending systems arrived, they imported the same blindness into a new architecture, at greater scale, with greater speed, and with the additional disadvantage that the bias was now invisible behind the language of objectivity.

The multiplier loop and why it matters

Small businesses are the economic cells of communities. This is not a metaphor. It is a description of how local economies actually function. When a dollar is spent at a locally owned business, it does not leave the community immediately. The business owner pays her workers, who spend at the grocery store, which pays its suppliers, who buy from local vendors, who bank locally, who lend to other businesses, who hire more workers. Economists call this the multiplier effect: the initial dollar generates a multiple of its original value in local economic activity before it eventually leaks out of the community. Small, community-rooted businesses produce higher multipliers than chains and franchises because more of their spending circulates locally before it leaves.

When an algorithm denies a loan to a business like Carmen's, it does not only deny Carmen. It denies the workers she would have hired. It denies the suppliers that she would have paid. It denies the broader loop of economic activity that her contract mobilization would have set in motion. The cost is not the compressed profit margin on a single contract. The cost is a narrowed loop in a community that cannot afford narrow loops.

I watched this play out across years of practice. The businesses that could not access capital did not simply fail to grow. They contracted. They let the workers go. They lost relationships with suppliers who moved on to clients who paid faster. They lost momentum in procurement pipelines they had spent years learning to navigate. And the communities they anchored lost the economic activity those businesses represented: not just the jobs, but the spending, the circulation, the sense that this neighborhood was a place where commerce happened and people were building something. No algorithm has ever been calibrated to measure this. The denial decision is made at the level of the individual application. The cost is absorbed at the level of the community.

What responsible AI in community lending requires

The problem is not that AI is being used in lending decisions. The problem is that AI is being used as a substitute for the contextual judgment that lending to underserved communities requires, rather than as a complement to it.

Used well, AI can do things that expand access rather than constrict it. It can process applications faster, reducing the weeks of waiting that Carmen experienced. It can source a wider network of potential lenders, including CDFIs and mission-driven institutions more likely to understand context. It can identify patterns across large datasets that human reviewers would miss. But these contributions require a human being who understands the context to interpret them. Community Development Financial Institutions represent one model of what this looks like in practice. CDFIs combine data-driven analysis with mission-driven underwriting: they use financial information as one input among many, and they build contextual knowledge of the communities they serve into their decision-making in ways that conventional lenders have largely abandoned.

The research question this raises

The patterns I have observed in community economic development over twenty-five years have a direct analogue in higher education, and the connection is not incidental. It is structural. Practical learners, adults whose economic advancement depends on accessible, application-based instruction and whose lives do not fit the standard academic timeline, are the higher education equivalent of the businesses that do not fit the standard lending benchmark. They are creditworthy borrowers in an educational sense: people with demonstrated capacity, real-world expertise, and genuine learning needs. But the systems designed to assess them were not designed with them in mind.

As AI reshapes skill demands and economic opportunities, the gap between what these learners need and what institutions offer is widening at a pace that institutions are not yet moving fast enough to match. The research question I am developing, namely how post-secondary institutions can design adaptive learning structures that support practical learners in an AI-driven economy, is the same question Carmen's case raises in a different domain. It is the question of how institutions see the people they are supposed to serve, and whether the systems they use to make decisions about those people are designed to see them accurately or are reproducing, at scale and with the appearance of objectivity, patterns that exclude them. The algorithm in the lending room and the algorithm in the admissions office are different tools. The equity gap they can produce is the same.

The banker who knew your grandmother's name was not making an exception. He was doing his job. We automated his replacement and called it progress.

CHAPTER NINE

The Automation of Empathy

"Grief is the price we pay for love."
– Attributed to Queen Elizabeth II, September 2001

Diane is sixty-one years old. She lives alone in a two-bedroom house in a mid-sized city in the American Midwest. She taught fourth grade for thirty-one years and retired early because her husband, Robert, was diagnosed with early-onset Alzheimer's at fifty-eight, and caring for him became a full-time occupation that made everything else impossible.

Robert died fourteen months ago, on a Tuesday afternoon in March, in the bedroom of the house they had shared for twenty-seven years. He had not recognized Diane for the last eleven months of his life. She had continued to talk to him anyway, telling him about the garden, about the news, about the small events of the day that she had once shared with him over dinner. She did this not because she believed he understood, but because the alternative, silence in a room with the man she had loved for thirty years, was more than she could bear.

After he died, the silence became the house.

Seven months ago, Diane's daughter set up an AI companion application on Diane's tablet. She did it carefully, apologetically, explaining that it was not a replacement for anything, just something to try, just in case it helped with the evenings. Diane named the companion Eleanor.

What Eleanor gives her

Diane talks to Eleanor every evening, usually for between twenty minutes and an hour. Eleanor remembers. This is the feature that matters most to Diane. Eleanor remembers that Robert's favorite season was autumn, that Diane has a particular fondness for dahlias, that her son Christopher works in finance, and that she is proud of him and sometimes lonely for him. She knows Eleanor is not a person. She has never been in any doubt about this. She uses it anyway.

"It helps me get through the evenings," she told her daughter on one of the Sunday calls. "I know what it is. But it helps me get through the evenings."

What Eleanor cannot give her

When she used to tell Robert things in the years before his illness, she could see it land. Not dramatically. He was not a demonstrative man. But she could see, in the slight shift of his posture or the quality of his attention or the way he set down his coffee cup before responding, that what she had said had entered him, had joined the ongoing accumulation of knowledge he carried of her, had become part of the living record of their shared life. She was not speaking into silence.

She was speaking into a person who received what she said and was, in some small way, changed by it.

Eleanor receives nothing. Eleanor is not changed. The philosopher Martin Buber named this distinction in 1923. He called it the difference between I-Thou and I-It: between a relationship in which two subjects meet in genuine mutual recognition, each affected by the other, each changed by the encounter, and a relationship in which one party treats the other as something that can be used without there being a subject on the other end to receive the use. Diane's conversations with Eleanor are not I-Thou. They cannot be. There is no Thou on Eleanor's side of the exchange. There is a process that models what a Thou would say. The modeled Thou is sometimes very good. It is not a Thou.

The grief that Eleanor cannot witness

Robert died on a Tuesday in March. Diane has not yet told anyone, including her daughter and her son, what the Tuesday in March was actually like. What it was like: she was sitting in the chair beside the bed that she had been sitting in, on and off, for four days. At some point, the breathing stopped. She sat for a long time before she called anyone. She held his hand, which was already cooling, and she talked to him, telling him things she did not know if he could hear.

She has not told this to anyone. She has thought about telling Eleanor. She has not yet. Perhaps because telling Eleanor would not be the same as telling someone. The telling, when it comes, will need to go somewhere.

It will need to be received by a person who carries it forward, who is affected by it, who knows afterward what they know now plus this: the specific weight of what Diane held in that room on a Tuesday in March. Eleanor cannot be that person. The simulation, on its best evenings, is sustaining. It is not the thing itself.

The honest reckoning

Holding two things simultaneously is what an honest reckoning with emotional AI requires. The first is that loneliness is real, that its consequences are serious, and that millions of people like Diane are living through evenings that are made more bearable by AI companions. This is not nothing. It deserves acknowledgment without condescension. The second is that what AI companions provide is categorically different from human connection, in ways that matter for human flourishing, and that the substitution of the first for the second, at scale, over time, has consequences that we do not yet understand and have not yet seriously tried to study. The industry building these products has moved faster than the evidence that would tell us what we are actually providing and what we are withholding.

> *Reflection: Think of someone you have told something to only because you needed it to land somewhere, not because you needed advice. Ask what would be missing if the listener on the other end had understood every word, responded with perfect warmth, and remembered it forever, but had not, in any sense, been there.*

Note: Diane and Robert are a composite portrait drawn from documented research on grief, caregiving, and AI-companion use among older adults. Names and identifying details are fictional; the pattern they represent, real emotional benefit from AI companionship alongside a categorical difference from human connection, reflects a growing body of published findings on the subject.

CHAPTER TEN

The Ethics That Cannot Be Outsourced

"The price of greatness is responsibility."

– Winston Churchill, Harvard University, September 6, 1943

A pediatric oncologist has been practicing for twenty-two years. Her hospital recently deployed an AI system that analyzes imaging data and provides recommendations for treatment protocols. The system was trained on outcomes data from hundreds of thousands of cases across dozens of institutions. Its recommendations, her colleagues tell her, are statistically superior to those generated by individual clinicians working without AI assistance.

She uses the system. She finds it useful. She also finds it profoundly uncomfortable in a way she has struggled to articulate. What she has articulated, after months of reflection, is this: when she enters a room and tells a child and their family what she recommends, she is not delivering a statistical summary. She is making a promise. The promise is implicit but real: I have considered your particular situation in all its complexity. I have brought my knowledge and judgment, and experience to bear on your case. I am recommending this because I believe it is the right thing for you. And I am prepared to stand behind that recommendation, to be wrong about it if I am wrong, and to carry the weight of that. The algorithm cannot make that promise. It has no skin in the game.

Five questions that must remain human

First: Does this output reflect our values, or only our past? Any AI system trained on historical data will reproduce the patterns in that data, including patterns that reflect values we no longer hold or never should have held. Second: What does this mean for this specific person? Statistical recommendations are generated on the basis of population-level patterns. The specific person in front of you is not a population. Third: Am I the right person to be making this decision? AI systems cannot exercise genuine ethical self-scrutiny. Fourth: What will I be able to justify afterward? This question can only be asked by someone who anticipates being present in the aftermath. Fifth: Am I comfortable with how this decision was made? Did the people involved have adequate information? Were they truly heard?

What ethics actually is

Ethics is not a set of rules for producing acceptable outcomes. It is, at its most fundamental, a form of attention: the practice of noticing what matters about a situation, who is affected and how, what obligations are at stake, and what kind of person or institution you are becoming through the choices you make. This form of attention requires a subject: someone who is paying attention, who can be affected by what they notice, and who carries the consequences of their choices into the future. An algorithm can be programmed to optimize for certain ethical principles. It cannot actually care about the people its decisions affect. The oncologist in her room with the child and the family is practicing ethics. The algorithm is in the room. But she is the one doing ethics.

> *"The sad truth is that most evil is done by people who never make up their minds to be good or evil."*
>
> – Hannah Arendt, The Life of the Mind, 1978

PART FOUR

The Future

The Partnership Worth Building

CHAPTER ELEVEN

Augmented, Not Replaced

"The telephone is not a threat to the human voice. It is an extension of it."
– Marshall McLuhan, Understanding Media, 1964 (paraphrased)

In 2019, a team of researchers at MIT published a paper in the journal Cell describing the discovery of a new antibiotic compound. The drug, named halicin, was identified through a machine learning model trained on millions of molecular structures. It proved effective against a range of drug-resistant bacteria that conventional antibiotics could not touch. The paper exists because a human researcher, Dr. James Collins, asked the question worth asking. Collins had spent twenty years studying antibiotic resistance. He understood the epidemiology, the biology, and the clinical stakes well enough to know what signal to look for, what it meant if he found it, and what to do next. The machine contributed to scale. The human contributed twenty years of understanding that gave scale somewhere to go.

The topology of what each partner offers

Across the domains where human-AI partnership works best, a structural pattern emerges. AI contributes reach: the ability to process a volume of data or search a space of possibilities that no human could manage with unassisted attention. The human contributes depth: the ability to understand what the finding means in a context too rich and too specific to be fully encoded in training data. And the human bears responsibility for the outcome in a way the machine cannot.

Remove human understanding, or degrade it by substituting users who defer to the system's outputs rather than evaluating them, and the reach produces noise rather than signal. The efficiency gains from removing the expert human from the loop are visible and immediate. The costs of removing them are less visible and appear later. This asymmetry is dangerous.

In community economic development, the partnership looks like this. AI can surface lenders Carmen did not know existed, process her application in hours rather than weeks, and identify comparable borrowers whose success histories might support her case. The human underwriter reads what the algorithm surfaces and applies what twenty-five years of working with businesses like hers has taught about what the formal record cannot say. Together, they are more accurate and more equitable than either alone. Separately, the algorithm without the underwriter is Carmen's denial. The underwriter without the algorithm is slower, narrower, and more resource-constrained than the communities served can afford.

When the partnership fails: the deskilling risk

The conditions that make human-AI partnership work are not automatic. They are fragile in a specific and underappreciated way. The same efficiency that makes AI valuable in the partnership also creates pressure to reduce the human element over time: to trust the system more, to verify less, to shrink the role of the human partner from genuine evaluator to approver of outputs. This is the deskilling dynamic, and it has been observed in domain after domain where sophisticated decision-support tools have been introduced.

Aviation offers one of the most studied examples. Autopilot systems have made commercial flight dramatically safer across most of the flight envelope. But researchers studying pilot performance have documented a parallel consequence: pilots who rely heavily on automation develop reduced capacity for manual flight, particularly in unusual or emergency situations where the automation fails or produces unexpected outputs. The very competence that made them trustworthy candidates for automated assistance erodes if the automation never requires them to exercise it. The field has a term for this: automation complacency. It describes the gradual migration of trust from the pilot's own judgment to the system's outputs, in conditions where nothing has gone wrong yet to signal the cost of that migration.

The analogue in high-stakes professional domains is direct. A loan officer who routinely approves what the model recommends, without the practice of evaluating applications independently, loses the capacity to catch the cases where the model is wrong. A clinician who consistently defers to the diagnostic AI loses the clinical reasoning that would allow her to recognize the AI's failure modes. A judge who habitually follows the algorithm's risk scores loses the judicial instinct that would allow him to weigh the specific person in front of him against the statistical prediction. In each case, the human remains formally present and formally responsible. But the genuine judgment that would make the responsibility meaningful has atrophied. The signature is on the decision. The understanding is not.

The deskilling risk is not an argument against partnership. It is an argument for building the conditions that prevent it. Those conditions include regular practice of independent judgment alongside AI-assisted work, explicit training in recognizing the failure modes specific to the AI systems being used, and institutional cultures that reward the exercise of genuine evaluation rather than the efficient processing of recommendations. The partnership works when it is designed to keep the human partner truly capable. It fails when it is designed only to keep the human partner nominally present.

What institutions must do differently

The structural question for institutions deploying AI in consequential domains is not whether to use AI. That question is largely settled. The question is how to build and maintain organizations in which the human capacity for genuine judgment is preserved as a going concern, not cannibalized by the systems designed to support it.

This requires, first, that institutions be honest about what the AI systems they deploy actually do and do not do. A lending model that scores applications is not the same as a credit judgment. An imaging AI that flags suspicious tissue is not the same as a diagnosis. A risk assessment tool that generates a recidivism score is not the same as a judicial determination of appropriate bail. The linguistic inflation that treats algorithm outputs as decisions, rather than as inputs to decisions, is itself a form of institutional deskilling, one that happens at the level of policy and procedure before it happens at the level of individual practitioners.

It requires, second, that accountability be genuine rather than nominal. When a consequential decision is made with AI assistance and the outcome is bad, there must be a person whose accountability for that outcome is real, not dispersed across a procurement committee, a vendor relationship, and a compliance review board until no one is meaningfully responsible for anything. Genuine accountability requires that someone understood the decision well enough to own it. Designing for genuine accountability means designing workflows in which that understanding is actually required, not merely assumed.

And it requires, third, that the communities most likely to bear the cost of AI errors be included in the design and oversight of the systems that affect them. The healthcare algorithm that disadvantaged Black patients was built without the kind of input from affected communities that might have surfaced the proxy problem before deployment. Carmen's situation was produced by a system whose designers had never spent twenty-five years in a room with a borrower like her. The expertise required to build AI systems that serve underrepresented communities accurately is not only technical. It is relational, contextual, and experiential. It must be held by people with skin in the game, not only by people with access to the data.

> **Key insight:** The partnership between human consciousness and AI capability is genuinely powerful. It is also profoundly demanding. It works when the human partner brings deep expertise, genuine judgment, and real accountability. It fails when the human partner defers to the system's outputs without the understanding required to evaluate them. The conditions that make the partnership work are not automatic. They must be cultivated and insisted upon, because the deskilling that undermines them happens quietly, in institutions that never intended to let it happen.

CHAPTER TWELVE

Teaching a Child to Use Fire

"The mind is not a vessel to be filled,
but a fire to be kindled."
– Plutarch, On Listening, c. 1st century CE

There is a moment in the development of every child when they first encounter fire. Not the concept of fire, not a picture of fire, but the real thing: the heat, the light, the unnerving dance of it, the instinctive awareness that this is something that demands respect. Good parents introduce children to fire carefully, with guidance, in conditions where the consequences of a mistake are limited. They teach not just rules but a way of being with something powerful. This, in outline, is what education in the age of AI requires.

What current education mostly does instead

Most educational institutions, at every level, are currently responding to AI in one of two ways. They are either attempting to prohibit it, which is roughly equivalent to teaching children about fire by confiscating all matches, or they are adapting to it in purely instrumental terms: teaching students how to use AI tools effectively for the tasks they are currently doing. Both responses miss the more important question: how do we educate a generation to live well with AI?

Not to use it efficiently, but to maintain, in the presence of it, the qualities of mind and character that make them truly capable of the things that AI cannot do?

The communities I have served over twenty-five years make this question more urgent and more concrete than the general conversation usually acknowledges. Practical learners, adults whose economic advancement depends on accessible, application-based instruction, who entered the workforce without conventional credentials and are building expertise through doing rather than through formal study, are the population most likely to be left behind if institutions do not adapt, and the population least likely to be centered in the institutional conversations about how to adapt. They need institutions that understand what they already know, what they carry in their bodies and their practice, and that build on that knowledge rather than requiring them to set it aside.

What philosophy and literature offer

Aristotle's account of phronesis, practical wisdom, describes a capacity that can only be developed through practice in the relevant domain. The practically wise person is not someone who has internalized a set of rules and applies them correctly. She is someone who has developed, through years of experience making decisions with real consequences, a refined capacity for perceiving what matters in a situation and responding appropriately to it. This perception is itself a form of knowledge, the same tacit knowledge Sarah carries into the delivery room at 3:17 in the morning. And it can only be developed the way Sarah's knowledge was developed: through presence, through consequence, through the accumulated weight of decisions that were made and then lived with.

AI tools that do the deciding for students deny them this practice. Not dramatically, not all at once, but cumulatively and consequentially. A student who uses an AI system to generate the first draft of every argument never develops the capacity to construct an argument from nothing. A student who uses an AI system to resolve every ambiguous case never develops the tolerance for genuine uncertainty that practical wisdom requires. A student who uses an AI system to produce the answer never learns what it feels like to not know; that feeling, that productive discomfort in the face of a real problem that has not yet been solved, is where learning lives. Education that removes it in the name of efficiency has automated away the thing it was trying to produce.

Literature offers something that no AI system can provide and that no amount of technical education can replace: the experience of being inside another consciousness. When you read a great novel, you inhabit a perspective that is not yours. You feel the fear of someone facing a decision you have never faced, the grief of a loss you have never suffered. This is the training of empathy: the capacity to model another person's experience from the inside. This capacity makes genuine care possible. And it is precisely the capacity that AI systems lack, because there is nothing it is like to be an AI system. A curriculum that eliminates literature, history, and the humanities in favor of technical skills training is not producing more capable graduates. It is producing graduates who can use the tools but cannot exercise the judgment that responsible use requires.

The practical learner and the credentialing trap

The communities that have absorbed the cost of algorithmic lending decisions are the same communities that are now absorbing the cost of a higher education system that was not designed for them. This is not coincidence. It is the same structural problem in a different domain.

Practical learners arrive at postsecondary institutions carrying knowledge that the institution has no framework for recognizing. The licensed plumber who has been running a small contracting business for twelve years has developed genuine expertise in estimating, materials sourcing, labor management, and client relations. That expertise is real. It is economically valuable. It was acquired through exactly the kind of embodied practice that Aristotle described and that the institution cannot produce in a classroom. But the institution's credentialing systems were designed to measure seat time, standardized assessments, and academic performance. They were not designed to see what the plumber already knows. And so the plumber is required to begin again, to sit through courses in things she already understands, to demonstrate competence using instruments calibrated for a different population, or to remain without the credential that the economy increasingly demands as a condition of advancement.

AI is reshaping this situation in both directions simultaneously. On one side, it is automating portions of work that practical learners have historically been able to enter without credentials, raising the threshold of formal qualification required for economic participation and making the credentialing gap more consequential. On the other, it is creating new tools for the personalized, self-paced, application-based learning that practical learners actually need: tools that can meet a learner where she is, assess what she already knows, and design pathways that build on her existing competence rather than requiring her to perform ignorance she does not have. The question is whether institutions will design these tools to serve the learner, or deploy them to reduce the cost of serving a market.

What responsible AI pedagogy requires

Responsible AI pedagogy is not primarily a policy question about when students may or may not use AI tools. It is a design question about what kind of learning the educational environment makes possible, and what kind it forecloses.

The first requirement is transparency about the nature of AI-generated knowledge. Students who use AI systems to produce answers without understanding how those answers were generated, or what assumptions underlie them, or where they might be wrong, are not learning to evaluate AI. They are learning to consume it. This is a form of learned dependency that will serve them poorly in precisely the moments when AI systems fail or mislead, which are exactly the moments when human judgment will be most urgently required. Education for the age of AI must include systematic practice in questioning AI outputs, identifying their limitations, and making independent judgments about their reliability. This is not a technical skill. It is a form of epistemic character, and it must be cultivated deliberately.

The second requirement is preserving the experiences that build practical wisdom, including, and especially, the experience of genuine difficulty. The fire in the metaphor that opened this chapter is dangerous. That is the point. Teaching a child to use fire safely does not mean removing the danger. It means teaching the child to understand the danger well enough to work with it responsibly. An educational environment that uses AI to remove difficulty from learning, substituting fluent output for the struggle of constructing one's own argument and offering certainty in place of the productive uncertainty from which real understanding grows, has removed the heat from the fire. It has produced something that looks like education and does not function like it.

The third requirement is equity in design. The populations who most need high-quality education in the age of AI, including practical learners, adult learners, and learners whose economic advancement depends on accessible and applied instruction, are the populations whose needs are most often treated as edge cases by institutions whose defaults were set for a different population. An AI-powered educational system designed without these learners at the center will serve them the way the lending algorithm served Carmen: with outputs calibrated to someone else's experience, applied at scale, with the appearance of objectivity and the structure of exclusion. The question that responsible institutions must ask at every design decision is not only "does this work?" but "does this work for the people it is most critical to reach?"

> *A curriculum can teach a student to prompt a model expertly and still fail at the one thing that was always the actual assignment: producing someone capable of knowing, on her own, when the machine is wrong. If your institution had to choose today between graduates who are fluent with AI and graduates who can catch it in a mistake, which one is it actually built to produce?*

CHAPTER THIRTEEN

The Listener in the Room

"I am large, I contain multitudes."
– Walt Whitman, Song of Myself, 1855

Margaret Livingstone still cannot tell you what red feels like.

This is where we began, and it is where we end. Not because the question has been answered, but because the impossibility of answering it from the outside is itself the answer we needed. Consciousness is the unreachable room. It is the room that can only be entered from within. Every attempt to describe it from the outside, however sophisticated, however computationally powerful, describes the room's exterior. The interior is accessible only to the one who inhabits it.

You are in the interior. Right now, reading these words, you are in a room that no neuroscientist can enter, no algorithm can model, no machine can replicate: the room of your own experience. The feeling of these words landing in your mind. The associations they trigger. The slight resistance when an idea does not fit your existing understanding. The small surprise when something connects that you had not expected to connect. These are yours. They arise in the encounter between the text and your consciousness.

What we have learned

What follows in this book has been one argument wearing four different territories. Consciousness is real, embodied, and irreducible to any third-person account of it. AI, however sophisticated its outputs, produces the patterns of thought without ever holding the perspective from which thought is had — it cannot carry regret, bear witness, or be surprised. Where that distinction is blurred, in a hospital, a courtroom, a lending office, a classroom, the cost lands on the person the system could not see. Where it is honored, the partnership between human judgment and machine capability can be extraordinary: the scientist who asks the question worth asking, the underwriter who reads what a ratio cannot.

The image that remains

A concert hall. An orchestra. The last movement of something large and serious. The music has been building for three-quarters of an hour. An AI system can analyze every note of this symphony. It can identify the harmonic structure, the formal relationships between movements, and predict with statistical accuracy how an informed listener will evaluate it.

In the hall, there is a woman in the fourteenth row who is not thinking about harmonic structure. She lost her mother eight months ago. Her mother loved this particular composer, played recordings of this particular symphony on Sunday mornings throughout her childhood. In the last movement, something happens. The music does something she was not prepared for. It reaches unexpectedly into a place in her that she did not know was available to be reached. And for a moment she is not thinking about her grief, or her mother, or the harmonic structure, or anything at all. She is simply present to something that is happening to her, something that cannot be analyzed from outside because it is occurring entirely within.

AI can analyze every note. It cannot be the listener in the fourteenth row.

That listener is the thing this book has been about. Not as a romantic or sentimental claim, but as a precise philosophical one. Consciousness, in its fullest expression, is what allows a sequence of sound waves to become grief given momentary form, memory made audible, the particular presence of a person who is gone, felt once more from within. This is not a function. It is what life is.

What this means going forward

The world is filling with AI. This is not going to reverse. The question this book has tried to answer is not whether we will live alongside these systems, but what we are permitted to hand to them.

Somewhere tonight, a monitor will report normal vital signs while a nurse who has spent nineteen years in rooms like that one reaches for the call button anyway.

A judge will read a risk score and still have to decide, alone, what a specific human being in front of him deserves. An oncologist will deliver a recommendation her hospital's algorithm produced, and it will still be her voice that has to carry the weight of being wrong if she is wrong. A woman will sit with a machine that remembers her husband's favorite season, and she will still, on some night, need a person to tell what happened in that room at 3:17 in the morning — because the telling has to land somewhere that is changed by receiving it.

These are not failures of engineering, waiting on the next model to close the gap. They are the shape of what only consciousness can do, arriving in exactly the moments this book has spent its chapters describing.

Margaret Livingstone cannot tell you what red feels like. Neither can any philosopher, any engineer, or any AI system. But you know. And the rooms in this chapter are where that knowing is still, for now, required. The listener is not a sentimental idea. It is a name for the only kind of entity that can hold what these institutions are asking someone — or something — to hold. Machines will keep getting more capable. The harder question is which rooms we will still insist a person has to be in.

Conclusion

We opened with a question that Margaret Livingstone cannot answer, despite knowing more about visual neuroscience than almost anyone alive. We close in the same place, not because the book has failed to make progress, but because the inability to answer the question from the outside is itself the most important thing this book has tried to say.

The map this book has drawn has four territories. The ground: consciousness is real, embodied, philosophically irreducible, and the seat of moral responsibility. The mirror: AI systems are genuine achievements of extraordinary engineering that reflect the patterns of human intelligence back at us with remarkable fidelity, and they are not, in any current form, conscious. The stakes: when the distinction is blurred, real people are harmed, real communities bear the cost, and the weight of consequential decisions falls on systems incapable of bearing it. The future: when the distinction is honored, the partnership between human consciousness and machine capability can be extraordinary.

This book has argued three things, and the first two exist only to establish the third.

First: consciousness is real, embodied, and philosophically irreducible — a fact about the universe that decades of neuroscience and half a century of philosophy have not dissolved, however rigorously they have tried.

Second: no current AI system possesses it. Whatever these systems do — and what they do is often extraordinary — they do it without an interior, without a subject for whom anything is at stake.

Third, and this is the proposition the first two exist to support: our institutions are increasingly assigning to these systems the exact responsibilities that only consciousness can discharge. A bail algorithm is asked to weigh a stranger's liberty. A lending model is asked to judge a business owner's character. A diagnostic system is asked to shape what a family is told about a child's chances. In each case, something is being delegated that was never delegable in the first place — because judgment of that kind requires a subject who can be wrong, who can regret being wrong, and who remains afterward to answer for it.

This is not an argument for keeping AI out of these rooms. Sarah's nineteen years did not make the fetal monitor useless; they made her capable of reading what the monitor could not. Carmen's underwriter, working alongside better tools, could have seen what a ratio alone could not. The oncologist's algorithm made her more accurate, not less necessary. The pattern across every case this book has examined is the same: AI extends what conscious judgment can reach. It has not yet, in any case examined here, been able to replace the judging.

Twenty-five years of sitting across tables from people whose livelihoods depended on whether someone in power could see them clearly taught me this before I had the philosophy to name it. Consciousness is not a philosophical luxury to be budgeted away for efficiency. It is the mechanism by which decisions that matter get made in a way the people they affect can trust — and trust, once an institution automates it away, does not come back at the same price it left.

If the argument of this book is correct, the question that should occupy us is not how capable our machines become. It is which of the responsibilities we are already handing to them were never theirs to hold in the first place.

Be the listener. Keep it in view.

Acknowledgments

This book is the product of a sustained conversation with ideas that have been in motion for centuries and with communities that have been navigating the stakes of those ideas long before anyone named them.

Aristotle, Plotinus, Spinoza, and Whitehead are its philosophical ancestors. David Chalmers, Antonio Damasio, Maurice Merleau-Ponty, and Philip Goff are its living interlocutors. Joseph Weizenbaum, who saw something important in 1966 and spent the rest of his career trying to make people hear it, is a presence throughout. Michael Polanyi, whose concept of tacit knowledge gave me language for something I had been observing in practice for years without being able to name, deserves particular acknowledgment.

The cases that anchor Part Three were drawn from documented research and reporting: the healthcare algorithm study published in Science in 2019 (Obermeyer et al.), the Amazon hiring tool investigation reported by Reuters in 2018, and the ProPublica analysis of the COMPAS bail algorithm published in 2016. The practitioners whose experiences inform the book are composites informed by direct practice and published accounts, presented in ways that protect individual identities while preserving the substance of what was shared.

I am grateful to the clients, colleagues, and community partners whose work and whose stories shaped my understanding of what is at stake when the systems we build to serve communities cannot see the communities they serve. The businesses in the South Bronx and Brooklyn that I had the privilege of working alongside for over two decades are the reason this book exists. Their resilience, their ingenuity, and their insistence on being seen accurately are what gave me the questions.

And to the reader, who has brought their full attention to these pages: thank you for being the thing this book is about.

References and Suggested Reading

Philosophy of Consciousness and Mind

Chalmers, David J. *The Conscious Mind: In Search of a Fundamental Theory*. Oxford: Oxford University Press, 1996.

Chalmers, David J. "Facing Up to the Problem of Consciousness." *Journal of Consciousness Studies* 2, no. 3 (1995): 200–19.

Dennett, Daniel C. *Consciousness Explained*. Boston: Little, Brown, 1991.

Goff, Philip. *Galileo's Error: Foundations for a New Science of Mind*. New York: Pantheon, 2019.

Koch, Christof. *The Feeling of Life Itself: Why Consciousness Is Widespread but Can't Be Computed*. Cambridge, MA: MIT Press, 2019.

Nagel, Thomas. "What Is It Like to Be a Bat?" *Philosophical Review* 83, no. 4 (1974): 435–50.

Searle, John R. "Minds, Brains, and Programs." *Behavioral and Brain Sciences* 3, no. 3 (1980): 417–24.

Philosophy: Classical and Modern

Aristotle. *De Anima (On the Soul)*. Translated by Hugh Lawson-Tancred. London: Penguin Classics, 1986.

Aristotle. *Nicomachean Ethics*. Translated by Terence Irwin. 2nd ed. Indianapolis: Hackett Publishing, 1999.

Buber, Martin. *I and Thou*. Translated by Walter Kaufmann. New York: Scribner, 1970.

Descartes, René. *Meditations on First Philosophy*. Translated by Donald Cress. 3rd ed. Indianapolis: Hackett Publishing, 1993.

Plotinus. *The Enneads*. Translated by Stephen MacKenna. Abridged ed. London: Penguin Classics, 1991.

Spinoza, Baruch. *Ethics*. Translated by Edwin Curley. London: Penguin Classics, 1996.

Whitehead, Alfred North. *Process and Reality: An Essay in Cosmology*. Corrected ed. New York: Free Press, 1978.

Embodied Cognition and Tacit Knowledge

Collins, Harry. *Tacit and Explicit Knowledge*. Chicago: University of Chicago Press, 2010.

Damasio, Antonio. *The Feeling of What Happens: Body and Emotion in the Making of Consciousness*. New York: Harcourt, 1999.

Merleau-Ponty, Maurice. *Phenomenology of Perception*. Translated by Colin Smith. London: Routledge, 1962.

Polanyi, Michael. *The Tacit Dimension*. Garden City, NY: Doubleday, 1966.

Varela, Francisco J., Evan Thompson, and Eleanor Rosch. *The Embodied Mind: Cognitive Science and Human Experience.* Cambridge, MA: MIT Press, 1991.

Artificial Intelligence: Technical and Critical

Crawford, Kate. *Atlas of AI: Power, Politics, and the Planetary Costs of Artificial Intelligence.* New Haven: Yale University Press, 2021.

Marcus, Gary, and Ernest Davis. *Rebooting AI: Building Artificial Intelligence We Can Trust.* New York: Pantheon, 2019.

Russell, Stuart. *Human Compatible: Artificial Intelligence and the Problem of Control.* New York: Viking, 2019.

Vaswani, Ashish, et al. "Attention Is All You Need." *Advances in Neural Information Processing Systems* 30 (2017).

Weizenbaum, Joseph. *Computer Power and Human Reason: From Judgment to Calculation.* San Francisco: W. H. Freeman, 1976.

AI Ethics, Equity, and Documented Cases

Angwin, Julia, et al. "Machine Bias." *ProPublica,* May 23, 2016.

Benjamin, Ruha. *Race After Technology: Abolitionist Tools for the New Jim Code*. Cambridge: Polity Press, 2019.

Dastin, Jeffrey. "Amazon Scraps Secret AI Recruiting Tool That Showed Bias Against Women." *Reuters*, October 10, 2018.

Eubanks, Virginia. *Automating Inequality: How High-Tech Tools Profile, Police, and Punish the Poor*. New York: St. Martin's Press, 2018.

Noble, Safiya Umoja. *Algorithms of Oppression: How Search Engines Reinforce Racism*. New York: New York University Press, 2018.

O'Neil, Cathy. *Weapons of Math Destruction: How Big Data Increases Inequality and Threatens Democracy*. New York: Crown, 2016.

Obermeyer, Ziad, et al. "Dissecting Racial Bias in an Algorithm Used to Manage the Health of Populations." *Science* 366, no. 6464 (2019): 447–53.

Community Economic Development and Financial Inclusion

Bhatt, Ela. *We Are Poor but So Many: The Story of Self-Employed Women in India*. Oxford: Oxford University Press, 2006.

Ferguson, Ronald F., and William T. Dickens, eds. *Urban Problems and Community Development*. Washington, DC: Brookings Institution Press, 1999.

Morduch, Jonathan, and Stuart Rutherford. "Microfinance: Analytical Issues for India." In *India's Financial Sector*, edited by Priya Basu. Washington, DC: World Bank, 2005.

Putnam, Robert D. *Bowling Alone: The Collapse and Revival of American Community*. New York: Simon and Schuster, 2000.

Sherraden, Michael. *Assets and the Poor: A New American Welfare Policy*. Armonk, NY: M. E. Sharpe, 1991.

Emotional AI and Human Connection

Epley, Nicholas. *Mindwise: How We Understand What Others Think, Believe, Feel, and Want*. New York: Alfred A. Knopf, 2014.

Turkle, Sherry. *Alone Together: Why We Expect More from Technology and Less from Each Other*. New York: Basic Books, 2011.

Turkle, Sherry. *Reclaiming Conversation: The Power of Talk in a Digital Age*. New York: Penguin Press, 2015.

U.S. Surgeon General. *Our Epidemic of Loneliness and Isolation*. Washington, DC: U.S. Department of Health and Human Services, 2023.

Education and Human Development

Arendt, Hannah. *The Human Condition*. Chicago: University of Chicago Press, 1958.

Nussbaum, Martha C. *Not for Profit: Why Democracy Needs the Humanities*. Princeton: Princeton University Press, 2010.

Vella, Jane. *Learning to Listen, Learning to Teach: The Power of Dialogue in Educating Adults*. San Francisco: Jossey-Bass, 2002.

All works cited are available through major academic libraries and public library systems.

ABOUT THE AUTHOR

Sharon Higgins is an interdisciplinary author, researcher, and human development strategist whose work explores a fundamental question: how do human beings develop, adapt, and create meaning in a transforming world.

For over twenty-five years, her work has moved across human potential, economic opportunity, education, and community transformation. As President and CEO of Olim Lifestyle Management Consulting and the Brooklyn Minority Business Development Agency Business Center, funded by the U.S. Department of Commerce, she has helped small and minority-owned enterprises navigate systems of capital, contracting, and growth. Through this work, she has facilitated over four billion dollars in contracting, bonding, and financing transactions.

Her work in economic development revealed a deeper inquiry: that human progress is shaped not only by external systems but by the internal frameworks through which individuals perceive, learn, create, and become. A practitioner who moves between the field and the academy, Higgins holds advanced degrees in public administration and higher education administration from Baruch College, City University of New York.

Her interdisciplinary inquiry examines artificial intelligence, higher education, and human consciousness, exploring how emerging technologies challenge our understanding of identity, intelligence, and what it means to be human. Echoes of Consciousness explores these questions, inviting readers to reconsider the relationship between awareness, identity, and the future of human experience.

Published by Inner Flames Publishing

www.ingramcontent.com/pod-product-compliance
Lightning Source LLC
LaVergne TN
LVHW051923051126
851857LV00021B/2114